This book belongs to

_____

First edition 2022
This edition published 2023 by
Ascension Publishing Group, LLC.

Copyright © 2022 Anno Domini Publishing
www.ad-publishing.co.uk
Text copyright © 2022 Suzy Senior
Illustrations copyright © 2022 Dubravka Kolanovic

Publishing Director: Annette Reynolds
Designer: Kev Holt, GingerPromo
Pre-production: Kev Holt, GingerPromo

Editorial review for Ascension by Amy Welborn.

Scripture passages are from the Revised Standard
Version—Second Catholic Edition © 2006 by the
Division of Christian Education of the National Council
of the Churches of Christ in the United States of
America. Used by permission. All rights reserved.

Ascension
PO Box 1990
West Chester, PA 19380
www.ascensionpress.com
1-800-376-0520

ISBN 978-1-954881-99-0

Printed in the United States of America
23 24 25 26 27 5 4 3 2 1

BASED ON THE PARABLE OF THE PRODIGAL SON
AND HIS BROTHER

The BEST HUG Ever

Written by
Suzy Senior

Illustrated by
Dubravka
Kolanovic

ASCENSION
Kids

West Chester, PA

Beaver was fed up with living in the lodge with his parents. He was tired of the babies pulling his tail.

He was bored with looking for food. And—as for the NEVER-ENDING building work—well, THAT was the last straw. Or twig.

5

"Dad," he announced, "I'm grown up now! I want to leave and do whatever I like!"

His father hugged him tightly. "I will miss you so much," he said, "but if that's what you want to do, I won't stop you."

"Great!" said Beaver. "Can I take my share of the food we've saved for winter, too?"

"Yes, Son," sighed his father.

So, the next morning, Beaver set off—all packed up with his share of sticks from the winter food store. He was so full of excitement, he didn't even look back.

But his family watched sadly, waving until Beaver was a tiny dot in the distance.

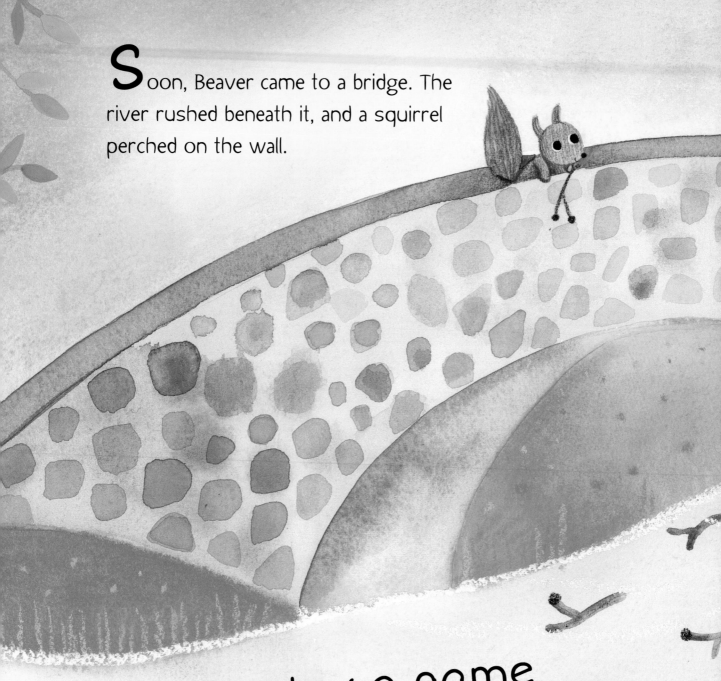

Soon, Beaver came to a bridge. The river rushed beneath it, and a squirrel perched on the wall.

"Let's play a game with the sticks!"

cried Beaver.

"I've got LOADS of sticks!"

And so, they did. They chose sticks from the food bag. Then dropped them—PLOP!—into the river, chasing them along to see which would win the race!

Beaver didn't even notice how many had gone. He was having SO much fun!

The next afternoon, Beaver passed some young deer having a party! They were nibbling on trees and laughing at jokes. Beaver REALLY wanted to join in.

"Hello!" he said.
The deer ignored him.

"Hmm," he thought, "I'm sure I'd be welcome if I brought food!" So, he pulled out all the best sticks and passed them around. By the time they had finished, the food bag was half empty! But Beaver didn't stop to worry—it was such a GREAT party!

SPLAT!

In the morning, Beaver traveled on. But suddenly—
SPLAT!—he stepped in a big, muddy bog.

"Ugh!" he gasped. "I'll have to go ALL the way
around this!"

14

Then he had an idea! He grabbed a bundle of sticks and scattered them across the mud. The winter food was really getting low—but Beaver didn't care.

Grinning, he skipped over the mud
on the little path he had made.

The weeks went by, and Beaver enjoyed his wild and carefree new life!

But then the nights grew colder, and ice crept over the bushes.

Finally, the snow settled, and food got VERY hard to find.

16

Beaver's tummy rumbled. "Ha! Time to start eating the winter food stores!" he decided.

But then he realized ... oh no!

All that was left in the bag were three small twigs. Beaver gnawed one hungrily.

The next week was even worse. And NONE of his new friends wanted to know him now that his sticks were all gone.

What COULD he eat? Snow? Too cold! Rocks? No, impossible!

Far from home, cold and hungry, Beaver thought of his
family back in the cozy lodge.

"Oh dear, oh dear," he wailed. "What have I done?"

At last, Beaver made a big decision: "I will go back," he thought. "I will tell Dad I'm sorry and say, 'I don't deserve to be treated like your son anymore.' Maybe he'll let me help with the hardest work in exchange for some food."

Nervously, he set off for home.

But ...
Guess what! Long before Beaver reached
the lodge, his father saw him in the distance!
He raced along the riverbank to meet him ...

"MY SON!"

he cheered … and he wrapped Beaver in the best hug EVER!

"I am so sorry!" sobbed Beaver. "I've let you down so badly. I don't even deserve to be your son anymore … "

Before Beaver could say any more,
his father had called the whole family
and all the neighbors!

"Bring him the best warm blanket!" he said. "Set out the very best food! I thought I had lost my son, but now he is found! Let's have a party and CELEBRATE!"

And so, they did! EVERYONE was happy ...

...Except for Beaver's big brother!
"I don't want to party," he grumbled. "HE went off and wasted everything, while I stayed here and did everything you asked me. Why does HE get a party? It's not fair."

His father took him gently by the paw and hugged him close.

"My son," he said, "I love you SO much. I always will. And EVERYTHING I have is yours. But I thought I'd lost your brother forever, and now he is home! Isn't that something to celebrate? Come! Let's be happy together."

THE PARABLE OF THE PRODIGAL SON AND HIS BROTHER

"**THERE WAS A MAN** who had two sons; and the younger of them said to his father, 'Father, give me the share of property that falls to me.' And he divided his living between them. Not many days later, the younger son gathered all he had and took his journey into a far country, and there he squandered his property in loose living. And when he had spent everything, a great famine arose in that country, and he began to be in want. So he went and joined himself to one of the citizens of that country, who sent him into his fields to feed swine. And he would gladly have fed on the pods that the swine ate; and no one gave him anything. But when he came to himself he said, 'How many of my father's hired servants have bread enough and to spare, but I perish here with hunger! I will arise and go to my father, and I will say to him, "Father, I have sinned against heaven and before you; I am no longer worthy to be called your son; treat me as one of your hired servants."' And he arose and came to his father. But while he was yet at a distance, his father saw him and had compassion, and ran and embraced him and kissed him. And the son said to him, 'Father, I have sinned against heaven and before you; I am no longer worthy to be called your son.' But the father said to his servants, 'Bring quickly the best robe, and put it on him; and put a ring on his hand, and shoes on his feet; and bring the fatted calf and kill it, and let us eat and make merry; for this my son was dead, and is alive again; he was lost, and is found.' And they began

to make merry. Now his elder son was in the field; and as he came and drew near to the house, he heard music and dancing. And he called one of the servants and asked what this meant. And he said to him, 'Your brother has come, and your father has killed the fatted calf, because he has received him safe and sound.' But he was angry and refused to go in. His father came out and entreated him, but he answered his father, 'Behold, these many years I have served you, and I never disobeyed your command; yet you never gave me a kid, that I might make merry with my friends. But when this son of yours came, who has devoured your living with harlots, you killed for him the fatted calf!' And he said to him, 'Son, you are always with me, and all that is mine is yours. It was fitting to make merry and be glad, for this your brother was dead, and is alive; he was lost, and is found.'"

-Luke 15:11-32

T his story is based on the parable of the Prodigal Son and his brother told by Jesus. You can find it in the Bible in Luke chapter 15, verses 11–32. (The real version has no beavers!) Hardly anyone understood why Jesus was interested in people who weren't "good" or who made mistakes. Jesus told this story to show that God is like a loving father who forgives us when we come back to ask for his help.